# ANGEL
# WORDS

# ALSO BY DOREEN VIRTUE

**Books/Kits/Oracle Board**
*The Angel Therapy® Handbook* (available January 2011)
*Archangels 101*
*The Healing Miracles of Archangel Raphael*
*The Art of Raw Living Food* (with Jenny Ross)
*Signs from Above* (with Charles Virtue)
*The Miracles of Archangel Michael*
*Angel Numbers 101*
*Solomon's Angels* (a novel)
*My Guardian Angel* (with Amy Oscar)
*Angel Blessings Candle Kit* (with Grant Virtue; includes booklet, CD, journal, etc.)
*Thank You, Angels!* (children's book with Kristina Tracy)
*Healing Words from the Angels*
*How to Hear Your Angels*
*Realms of the Earth Angels*
*Fairies 101*
*Daily Guidance from Your Angels*
*Divine Magic*
*How to Give an Angel Card Reading Kit*
*Angels 101*
*Angel Guidance Board*
*Goddesses & Angels*

## Audio/CD Programs

*Angel Therapy® Meditations*

*Archangels 101* (abridged audio book)

*Fairies 101* (abridged audio book)

*Goddesses & Angels* (abridged audio book)

*Angel Medicine* (available as both 1- and 2-CD sets)

*Angels among Us* (with Michael Toms)

*Messages from Your Angels* (abridged audio book)

*Past-Life Regression with the Angels*

*Divine Prescriptions*

*The Romance Angels*

*Connecting with Your Angels*

*Manifesting with the Angels*

*Karma Releasing*

*Healing Your Appetite, Healing Your Life*

*Healing with the Angels*

*Divine Guidance*

*Chakra Clearing*

## DVD Program

*How to Give an Angel Card Reading*

# ANGEL
# WORDS

## Visual Evidence of How
## Words Can Be Angels in Your Life

 DOREEN VIRTUE AND GRANT VIRTUE

**HAY HOUSE, INC.**
Carlsbad, California • New York City
London • Sydney • Johannesburg
Vancouver • Hong Kong • New Delhi

*Published and distributed in the United States by: Hay House, Inc.:* www.hayhouse.com • *Published and distributed in Australia by:* Hay House Australia Pty. Ltd.: www.hayhouse.com.au • *Published and distributed in the United Kingdom by:* Hay House UK, Ltd.: www.hayhouse.co.uk • *Published and distributed in the Republic of South Africa by:* Hay House SA (Pty), Ltd.: www.hayhouse.co.za • *Distributed in Canada by:* Raincoast: www.raincoast.com • *Published in India by:* Hay House Publishers India: www.hayhouse.co.in

*Editorial supervision:* Jill Kramer • *Project editor:* Alex Freemon • *Design:* Jenny Richards

**Library of Congress Cataloging-in-Publication Data**

Virtue, Doreen.
 Angel words : visual evidence of how words can be angels in your life / Doreen Virtue and Grant Virtue.
    p. cm.
 Includes bibliographical references.
 ISBN 978-1-4019-2696-0 (tradepaper : alk. paper) 1. Language and languages--Miscellanea. 2. Spiritual life. I. Virtue, Grant. II. Title.
 BF1999.V49 2010
 130.1'4--dc22

                              2010021579

**Tradepaper ISBN:** 978-1-4019-2696-0
**Digital ISBN:** 978-1-4019-2944-2

13  12  11  10    4  3  2  1
1st edition, November 2010

Printed in China

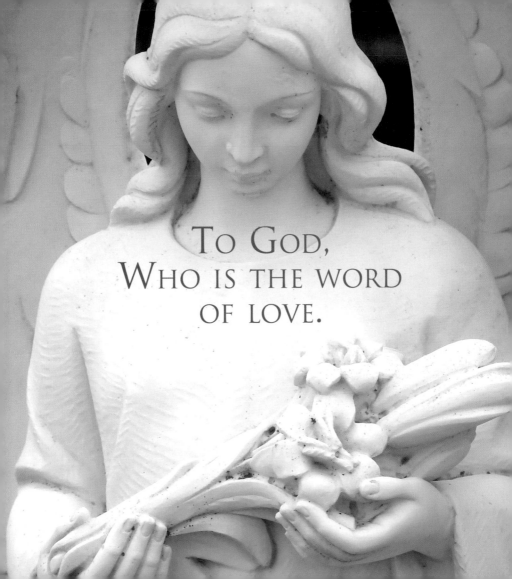

To God,
Who is the word
of love.

# CONTENTS

# INTRODUCTION

## by Doreen Virtue

*"Pleasant words are as an honeycomb,*
*sweet to the soul, and health to the bones."*

— Proverbs 16:24

When my son Grant and I were recording a podcast about archangels, he stopped and pointed to his computer screen, exclaiming, "Look! When you said the word *angel,* the graph made angel wings!" Sure enough, his computer program showed all sorts of shapes representing each word I'd used. And when I said "angel," the graph looked like a celestial being soaring from heaven:

Grant and I began experimenting with other words to find literal graphic representations of their meanings. What we discovered was remarkable: the words we consider positive and feel-good were significantly "larger" than those considered negative.

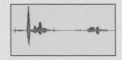

*Graphs of the spoken words* admiration *and* jealousy.

We were astounded by this visual representation of positive and negative utterances! Here was tangible evidence of high and low vibrations within speech. The positive words exhibited a much bigger impact, like light shining radiantly. Meanwhile, the negative ones looked tight and constricted.

The word *admiration* shows evidence of big radiant energy, while *jealousy* shows the opposite. This makes sense, since when you admire someone, you're affirming that there's abundance in the world. You're saying, "Wow, isn't it wonderful that this person is enjoying success, health, love, and happiness. If he or she can do this, then so can I!" Doesn't that feel expansive and generous?

Contrast this with the word *jealousy,* which is based upon a belief in lack and limitation. Jealousy says, "Hey! How come that person gets to have fun? How come I can't have what he or she has?" and "This isn't fair!" Can you feel the underlying fear within jealousy? No wonder it shows up as a small graph!

This very message was demonstrated during one of my appearances on the *Oprah* television show. My book *Losing Your Pounds of Pain* had just been released; and Oprah, her guests (including me), and the audience were discussing the psychology of weight loss and gain. This was in the early 1990s, when the talk-show host had lost a great deal of weight while working with a personal trainer and a personal chef.

Oprah's staff had collected and divided letters she'd received into two categories: (1) those from viewers who admired her weight loss and said that it inspired them to take up

this goal themselves, and (2) those expressing jealousy about her accomplishment. A sampling of the letter writers of both viewpoints had been flown in to the studio.

What Oprah discovered was remarkable: those who admired her weight loss had all been subsequently successful with a fitness, exercise, and weight-loss plan. Conversely, those who were jealous reported that they hadn't been able to lose even one pound! Clearly, this negative emotion blocked them from emulating Oprah's healthy habits. Their negative mind-sets wouldn't allow them to follow her positive example.

Similarly, a woman named Sharon Gartner (a reader of my books who contacted me) found that her smoldering jealousy of her neighbors blocked her from living the lifestyle that she desperately wanted. She'd look at others' nice houses and cars and say, "It's not fair! I never have enough of anything!"

Sharon felt as if she were living in a dark hole of despair and worry. She told me, "My thoughts and words were the shovel digging my way deeper into darkness." Sharon was so consumed with jealousy and loathing for those who had more than she did that she hadn't noticed that her husband had become withdrawn and moody and her children were unhappy. Nothing seemed to be going right in her family's life.

One night, Sharon had a dream of sitting on a park bench under a tree. A man who looked like a hobo sat beside her and handed her a piece of paper, which simply read: "Let it go." Sharon awoke with the knowledge that everything would be okay. She started affirming, "I give love and I receive love," and "I am open to receiving prosperity from expected and unexpected sources."

Sharon now describes her life as wonderful. She and her husband have fallen back in love and feel that they are living their dreams together. Wonderful opportunities come to them daily, and their children are now happy. Why? Sharon says: "It's because I changed my thinking pattern, guided by those three simple words: *Let it go.* I now realize that the reason my life wasn't going well was because my dark, jealous belief was that I wouldn't have 'nice things,' since I thought I wasn't worthy of having such things. I now live in a constant state of love and joy, with the knowledge that I am only open to receiving all that is good in my world."

 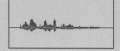

*When Sharon was jealous of others, she used low-energy phrases such as "It's not fair"* [graph on left] *and "I never have enough of anything"* [graph on right], *which resulted in happiness eluding her.*

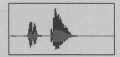  

*After Sharon had a dream in which she was told "Let it go"* [graph on left], *she began affirming, "I give love and I receive love"* [middle graph] *and "I am open to receiving prosperity from expected and unexpected sources"* [graph on right].

When you see someone who seems to have more than you do, you can either say, "Wow, I can do that, too!" or "Why don't I have that?" Hopefully, the graphs, stories, and discussions in this book will help you choose the former instead of the latter.

## Angel Words

Positive words, like guardian angels, can help you soar into new horizons. The mere act of altering your vocabulary and using life-affirming language can quickly and dramatically change your life in magical ways!

I'd always noticed my unpleasant reactions whenever I or others around me engaged in negative discussions. No matter how juicy the gossip, I can feel my stomach tightening in response to talking about others. The same goes for fear-based speculations about the earth's environment or humankind's future.

Looking at the constricted, negative word graphs, I could little wonder why my body feels tense around negative words! Low-vibrational conversations are *palpable!* In addition to stomach tightening, I notice that my energy and enthusiasm becomes drained. I'm tired and no longer smiling after a negative discussion. I remember a saying that someone wise taught me as a child: "Small people talk about other people, average people talk about material things, and great people talk about ideas." The adage is a bit blunt, but you get the idea.

Even the very words *negative* and *positive* show their different vibrations in graph form:

*Here's what the energy of the word* negative *looks like.*

*Compare the higher energy of the word* positive.

In my books and workshops, I frequently discuss how our positive thoughts attract and create positive life experiences. Most people understand this concept. Putting it into practice is another thing, and is a big part of personal growth. Positive living involves choosing corresponding words, a lesson I learned firsthand many years ago.

As a busy mother of two young sons, I rarely had time to think about my own wants or feelings. Mostly I was focused upon keeping my husband happy and attending to my children's needs. Like many young families, we had financial challenges, and some days I didn't know how we'd afford our electricity and food. So my mental atmosphere was filled with stress and fear.

At some point, I was given a book by Norman Vincent Peale called *Positive Imaging,* about the power of positive thinking. Peale explained how our affirmations need to be infused with gratitude, as if our wishes have already come true. So I created my own affirmations tape filled with my desires, such as "I am a best-selling author," "I am confident," "I have a healthy, physically fit body," "I have wonderful friends," and so forth.

Although these statements initially felt fictitious and false, I faithfully listened to them three times a day. I'd be vacuuming the rug with my earphones on, listening to the affirmations. And somewhere along the line, they sank in!

I clearly remember the day when the positive words "clicked": I was standing in line at the store, patiently waiting to buy food for my family. A man cut in front of me. Previously, I would have silently done nothing, and probably resented the man for usurping my place in line. But the affirmations tape shifted something deep inside of me, and I simply said, "Excuse me, but I was next."

The man turned to look at me as if seeing me for the first time. He apologized, and I took my turn—a huge victory for me personally, in that I stood up for myself, which I hadn't ever done before. The words on the tape helped me honor and value myself and my time.

From there, magic happened. Everything I'd affirmed came true, in almost miraculous ways. Of course, I had to put human effort into writing the books that eventually became bestsellers, and into the daily exercise and healthy eating that enabled me to have a fit body. But I credit the positive words on those tapes for giving me the confidence and courage to do the work!

In this book, Grant and I use a "positive picture is worth a thousand words" approach to illustrate the energy of words. He recorded all of the words on the graphs, and I wrote the text surrounding them.

Working on this book has made Grant and me acutely aware of the distinction between positive and negative words. Of course, we realize that there are contexts wherein some are positive to one person and negative to another. This is a topic we'll delve into within these pages.

To rule out the possibility that Grant's subjective feelings about each word were affecting the graph, he took two that are universally accepted as positive *(love)* and negative *(hate)* and recorded each while purposely feeling the same series of four successive emotions: *indifference, anger, interest,* and *joyfulness.*

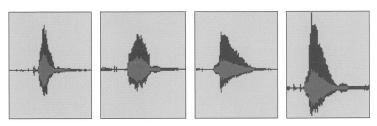

*The word* love, *spoken with four different emotions:*
indifference, anger, interest, *and* joyfulness.

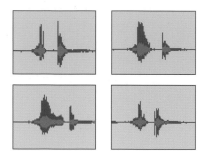

*Although the word* hate *was spoken by the same person, with the identical emotions, it still yields a much "smaller" graph. This shows that words carry an innate positive or negative essence, regardless of our subjective feelings about them.*

As you can see, while the words' sizes did fluctuate in response to Grant's varied emotions, *love* overall is significantly "larger" than *hate.* There's an essential positive energy infused into it, and an essence of negativity built into the contrasting word.

Some words, as you'll see in Chapter 7, can be either negative or positive depending upon the context in which they're used. Words such as *junk, plaguing,* and *fat* can be used to describe something pleasant or unpleasant. Interestingly, *drugs* has a large-energy graph (positive), but *addiction* has a very small-energy (negative) one.

When I look at the graphs, I can see how vocalizing each word sends lines of energy out into the world. When a positive word such as *love* is said, it emits a starburst of radiant energy; whereas a negative antonym *(hate)* is Scrooge-like and doesn't contribute anything of value to the world.

The number one question I'm asked during my workshops, on my radio show, and in my readers' letters is: "What is my life purpose?" I can heartily say that the graphs within this book hold the answer: *your purpose is to speak, think, and write the powerfully positive words that are so abundantly available to you.*

As a writer, I've always found that there's a positive and a negative way to say the same message. For instance:

*Graph of the phrase "You shouldn't say negative words . . ."*

*Graph of "Saying positive words can help you to feel happy."*

Although both sentences in the above graphs convey the same meaning, their energies are completely different. As you read the two phrases, how did they affect you? Did you notice any muscles tightening or relaxing in response to each? Which sentence feels better to you?

Before I submit a new book to my editor at Hay House, I scan for any sentences that can be rewritten in a more positive way. Each time I do so, I can feel the entire manuscript's energy level being uplifted. When the book consists of sentences that are written in affirmative tenses, its energy practically floats in the clouds!

It's like the old adage about people who view the same glass of water as being half-full or half-empty. Sure, they're saying the same thing, but who's having more fun?

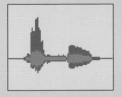  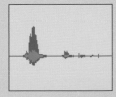

*Graphs of the phrases "Half-full" [left] and "Half-empty" [right].*

## Judgment vs. Discernment

When I say that a word is negative, I'm not implying that it's "bad" or "wrong." That is judgment, which is the ego's way of labeling and pigeonholing everything. Instead, the word *negative* is a synonym for *low-vibrating*.

While the ego relies on up-in-the-head judgment to decide whether something is good or bad, the higher self uses discernment, which is a feeling-based way of either being attracted to or repelled by something. Ego uses labels. The higher self employs feelings and the Law of Attraction.

As an example, the ego would say that cigarette smoking is bad. The higher self would say that it's not *attracted* to cigarette smoking. Which feels better, the ego's judgment or the higher self's discernment?

As Grant says: "The purpose of this book isn't to create some sort of verbal tyranny where you have to closely guard your speech. We simply would like to illustrate, in the plainest possible way, that what you say and how you say it can and does have an effect upon you and your environment. The vibrations of your voice go out and have the potential to subtly change everything they come in contact with.

"Once you have that critical piece of information, it then becomes your choice to use your words as you see fit. What I've learned from the research we've conducted in this book is that what I say can directly affect the outcome of any endeavor I am currently working on. I, for one, will certainly strive to ensure my speech is much more positive in the future."

Most likely, you can feel the effect that words have upon you. Your body's muscles tense as you read, think, write, or say negative ones, just as their tight, small graphs would suggest. Positive words, in contrast, help your muscles relax and your mind and heart open to loving energies.

In addition to these subjective effects, science is studying the impact that words have upon health and mental function, as you'll read when you turn the page.

# CHAPTER ONE

# THE STUDY OF WORDS

*"For attractive lips, speak words of kindness.
For lovely eyes, seek out the good in people. . . .
For poise, walk with the knowledge that
you will never walk alone."*

— SAM LEVENSON
(as quoted by Audrey Hepburn)

Words are composed of sounds, which have long been studied for their impact upon objects in the material world, including the human body. Pythagoras, the 6th-century B.C. Greek philosopher, played particular notes on stringed musical instruments to heal physical and emotional maladies. Since Pythagoras's time, thousands of scientific studies have correlated music with health.

For example, an 18th-century German physicist and musician named Ernst Chladni poured sand on metal plates. He then experimented with the shapes that it formed as he moved his violin bow across the plates.

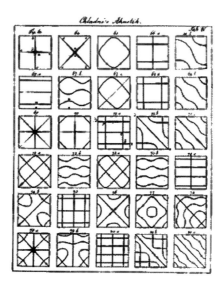

*Chladni's plates of sand showed the different shapes that various sounds make.*

Chladni's sound experiments have been replicated and expanded upon by other scientists using various powders and fluids, with equally exciting results. Most recently, Masaru Emoto's work has revealed how water molecules transform in response to the energy of positive and negative written words placed next to them.

Medical and behavioral-science studies also show the impact of words. An American medical anthropologist named W. Penn Handwerker studied 355 women's childhood histories. Handwerker found that those women who had been on the receiving end of childhood accusations that began with "you" (such as "You are stupid") were more likely to develop depression in adulthood. He also correlated this form of depression with the development of serious illnesses and addictions. Handwerker says that brain development is altered among children who are exposed to verbal violence. Clearly, negative words can hurt.

Another fascinating study showed that merely *reading* negative words can trigger the brain's pain centers. Thomas Weiss, a psychology professor at Germany's Friedrich-Schiller University of Jena, concluded: "Words alone are capable of activating our pain matrix."

Dr. Weiss used magnetic resonance tomography to scan the brains of subjects while they read pain-related words such as *tormenting, grueling,* and *plaguing.* The brain's pain centers were activated even when subjects were distracted while reading. Interestingly, as subjects read negative words not correlated with pain—such as *terrifying, horrible,* and *disgusting*—their pain centers *weren't* activated.

  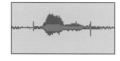

*Words that trigger the brain's pain centers appear very tight, small, and constricted on the graphs.*

Highly sensitive people can feel the energy of newspapers and newsmagazines that contain pain- and fear-related words. Some experience discomfort just being in the presence of these media outlets, so they avoid the news altogether.

The impact of words has long been known to medical personnel. A recent study in China supported the need for patients to only hear positive words (or even no words) following surgery. More than 600 post-hysterectomy patients were put into four groups according to the type of words that would be used by nurses who delivered their post-surgical morphine: negative words, mostly negative words, no words, or positive words.

The patients who received the all-negative words from their nurses also needed the most medication and showed other signs of increased pain compared to the other groups. The patients who received mostly negative words also fared worse than

those who received none or only positive ones. The effects were particularly significant immediately following surgery and seemed to lessen as the patients healed and grew stronger.

This study shows that those who are vulnerable because their health or energy is in a weakened condition are impacted by words the most.

The consensus is that doctors' and nurses' words during surgery can impact patients' health. This is based upon multiple studies showing that patients recall words spoken to them while being operated upon. For example, researchers in a Sheffield, England, hospital read words to 65 patients who were undergoing procedures under anesthesia. The patients recalled the words to a significant degree, indicating that the brain is receptive and sensitive to speech during anesthesia. This study was a replication of earlier ones that had yielded similar results.

If that's not enough, a recent study also shows that our brains register negative words *faster* than positive ones. Apparently, this is a survival mechanism to help us sense and avoid danger. In the study, University College London researchers showed negative, positive, and neutral words to subjects for a fraction of a second.

The subjects were correctly able to identify negative words much more than positive or neutral ones.

The positive words included *cheerful, peace,* and *flower:*

 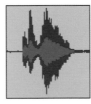 

The negative words included *murder, despair,* and *agony:*

The neutral words included *box, kettle,* and *ear:*

As you can see, the negative words have the smallest and most constricted graphs. Perhaps they act like stinging arrows that impact us faster than the larger, "slower-moving" words.

## THE SUBJECTIVITY OF WORDS

Our research found that words that are universally considered negative showed the smallest and most constricted graph patterns. Those that are subjective—negative to some people, and neutral to others—were smaller than those considered universally positive, but they still weren't quite as small as the universally negative ones.

For example, the word *drugs* can have positive connotations to some people who view these substances as helpful instruments of health or even feel-good recreation.

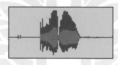

The word *drugs* appears smaller than the universally positive *love,* which almost rhymes with it (to eliminate speculation that the vowel sounds could influence graph size). Notice how far the graph extends for the word *love,* showing the high amount of energy that it exudes.

The word *addiction* implies the word *drugs*, but takes it to an unambiguously negative level. This negativity is represented by the tight, constricted graph:

Our gender and personality have a big impact on whether we view a word as negative, neutral, or positive. For example, several studies have also shown that women with eating disorders are emotionally triggered by words associated with a poor body image. Researchers scanned brain patterns of eating-disordered women while they heard unpleasant terms and phrases such as: *obesity, corpulence, buxom, thick, fatty, gain weight, heavy, chubby,* and *stumpy.* These words created measurable effects on the emotional-regulation part of the brain in women.

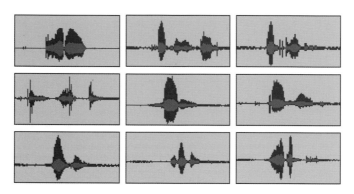

*Studies show that words associated with poor body image trigger the emotional center of the brain in eating-disordered women.*

In a follow-up study with men, however, the words only registered in their cognitive (thinking) brain region, not in their emotions.

Some people have stronger reactions to negative words than others. For instance, those with "borderline personality" traits (strong fears of abandonment, impulsiveness, chronic relationship issues, and so on) have a more intense startle reaction when shown unpleasant words, compared with people with nonborderline personalities.

In one study, people both with and without borderline personality traits heard a loud noise while reading negative words (like *hate, lonely,* and *abandon*) and while reading neutral ones (for example, *actually, collect,* and *regular*). Those with borderline personality reacted to the startling noise much more strongly when reading negative words, compared to when reading neutral ones. Those without borderline personality didn't react to the noise any differently under the two conditions.

What is a negative word to one person may be positive to someone else, based upon their individual personalities and their personal experiences. During the many years I've been giving workshops, for instance, I've noted how the name Jesus brings benevolent smiles to some audience members' faces and uptightness to others. To some, Jesus signifies the experience of pure love. To others, he is associated with fear, guilt, negative religious experiences, or prayer that seemed unanswered. Same name, different reactions.

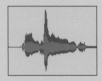

*The name Jesus has a large energy graph, although reactions to his name can vary according to personal experience with religion.*

The scientific studies about words are exciting and enlightening. You can conduct your own experiments by saying different words one at a time and noticing your body's reactions. Just as you wouldn't eat foods that have previously left you with indigestion, becoming aware of how various words affect you can help you choose them wisely.

   In the next chapter, we'll look at how saying positive words and phrases can change your life in exciting ways.

# CHAPTER TWO

# ANGEL WORDS FOR HELPING YOUR CAREER AND FINANCES

*"May you have warm words on a cold evening."*

— IRISH BLESSING

In this chapter, you'll meet some folks who have had dramatic positive experiences in their careers and finances simply by adopting more positive words in their everyday vocabulary. Their stories illustrate how positive words are like guardian angels that lead us onto higher pathways.

## Positive Words for Career and Finances

I receive a lot of calls for help through my Websites, radio show, and workshops. Frequently, I'm asked for angelically based answers to help resolve stressful financial and career situations. Invariably, I find that people—because of their stress—are using negative words to describe their current situation. They're often unaware that they're saying negative affirmations (such as "I'm broke") or that these statements are ensuring that their stressful condition will continue.

A woman named Carolyn Purchase has owned a metaphysical store in Nova Scotia for five years. In the past, whenever anyone would ask her how business was, she'd always reply, "I'll never be rich, but it pays its bills." Carolyn said that phrase countless times before realizing its impact.

One day she was chatting with a close friend about how the store should be a gold mine, since it's the only one in the region, with lots of customers and a great reputation. They wondered, then, why wasn't the store doing better? Why was it only making enough for Carolyn to buy inventory and pay the bills?

Carolyn got her answer when a customer asked how the store's business was doing. Just as she was about to give her standard, "I'll never be rich . . ." reply, she had an epiphany and said instead, "Fantastic! This place is a gold mine!" She said it with such conviction that she believed every word.

That was a year ago, and whenever anyone asks, "How's business?" Carolyn continues to say that it's fantastic and the place is a gold mine. In the last year, her sales have increased 40 percent over where they were the previous one . . . and they just keep climbing! All that has changed are Carolyn's words—from limiting ones to those with a positive energy vibration. Her words have *made* the gold mine.

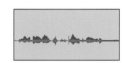

*In the past when Carolyn was asked how her business was,*
*she'd always reply, "I'll never be rich, but it pay its bills."*
*You can see here how small this statement's energy is.*

*Now Carolyn answers queries about how her store is doing by saying,*
*"Fantastic! This place is a gold mine!" and her profits*
*have risen 40 percent as a result.*

The words we say have a direct impact upon our finances, as Carolyn's story illustrates. And a woman named Livia Maris Jepsen went through a similar transition. A few years ago, Livia wondered why her prayers were only answered with "just enough," and never more. For instance, if she needed money to pay for something, she'd receive just the amount she required, and not a dime more. If she needed a little longer to finish something, she'd get just enough time complete it at the very last minute . . . and so on.

One day Livia visited a prosperous friend at the woman's mother's house. After serving her delicious meal, the mother asked, "Do you have enough?" and the friend answered, "Oh yes, Mom, I have plenty!" That was exactly what Livia needed to hear! She realized that she was always asking for and affirming "just enough."

Livia says, "If you ask the angels for just enough, that's exactly what you get. Try asking for 'plenty' and affirming 'plenty' and you'll always get much better than what you expect." Since changing her vocabulary, Livia is much more financially secure.

*When Livia prayed to receive "just enough," she was
barely earning sufficient income to cover her bills.*

*When Livia began praying for "plenty" of everything,
the energy of her words and her life expanded to new high levels.*

If asking for plenty of money creates discomfort, rest assured that you can use this extra cash for charitable contributions, helping your loved ones, and financing your Divine life purpose. Your increased flow allows you to give in even bigger ways!

Diana Mey is another woman who learned the power that words can have upon one's finances. Most of her life, she would say, "I don't have enough money for . . ." this or that. Diana's continual negative affirmations ensured that she'd never be able to afford anything she wanted.

Then Diana started seeing the number 818 repeatedly—on clocks, on license plates, in telephone numbers, and on receipts. She finally found the reason in my book *Angel Numbers 101*, which lists the meaning behind repetitive number sequences. The book explained that 818 was an angelic message to stay positive about money, and suggested that people who see this number use this affirmation: "I am financially secure now, and I have a surplus of money to spare and share."

Diana started saying this affirmation repeatedly, and today she is financially secure, with plenty to spare and share. She told me, "I now look at the world totally differently when it comes to money."

*Diana would say, "I don't have enough money for that"*
*repeatedly, and so created that situation for herself.*

*Here is Diana's new affirmation:*
*"I am financially secure now, and I have a surplus of money to spare*
*and share," which came true quickly for her.*

When I wrote a monthly column for a bookstore-owner trade magazine, I received many letters from people in dire financial situations. Invariably, they'd tell me that the city in which they had a bookstore wasn't a good place for a business. So I'd counsel them to please use positive words to describe the economy of their community (and the world in general). If you *say* the economy is bad, what sort of effect do you suppose that has upon it?

A woman named Lorraine Mills discovered that her negative affirmations about the city she lived in had negative effects on her business. When Lorraine moved to Japan from her native England, she kept saying that there wasn't a sufficient customer base in her new location to support her holistic therapy venture. Sure enough, Lorraine's business—which had thrived in the U.K.— slowed to a trickle. After several years of difficulties, Lorraine planned to return to England.

She made a business plan and visualized having a busy, full therapy practice when she returned to the U.K. Interestingly, though, that's when customers started coming to her practice in Japan! Lorraine realized that her negative affirmations about the local economy had pushed away business. She told me, "I had affirmed there were no customers for my therapy practice in Japan, so that's what I got." When she visualized success, it was like rolling out a red carpet at her business's front door.

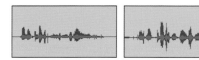

*When Lorraine complained, "There are no customers in this area" and "There is no customer base here," her low-energy words created the very thing she feared most.*

*Lorraine's new high-energy affirmation "It's easy to have a flow of abundance in this city" ensured that her business would be successful wherever it was located.*

Sometimes, a painful situation will wake us up to the role that our vocabulary is playing, as a woman named Caryn Connolly discovered. After she was laid off from her engineering job,

she started telling people, "I am unemployed." Caryn desperately searched for a new job, without success. Then she realized that by continually saying that she unemployed, she was *creating* that situation. So she stopped using that word, and shortly afterward, she was offered an engineering position that would pay all of her bills. Caryn says, "By changing the words I was using with myself and others, I was able to manifest abundance very quickly into my life."

Caryn didn't say positive words or affirmations. She simply *stopped* saying the negative affirmation "I am unemployed" . . . and everything changed.

*When Caryn said, "I am unemployed," she was affected by the statement's tight and small energy. It was a negative affirmation, which ensured that she'd continue to stay jobless. But when she stopped using these words, she was offered a wonderful position.*

Like Caryn, a man named Gabriel improved his career path by changing his vocabulary. Gabriel was in his last semester of graduate school; and he was ready to accept his degree, get his counseling license, and move on with his life. Because he was tired of school, he approached his upcoming licensing examination with a negative mind-set.

Gabriel said to himself, "This test is silly," and "I don't think I am smart enough." Not surprisingly, he failed his exam. He realized that his own negative words had been the cause, so he decided to use more positive ones.

As he studied for his second attempt, Gabriel used positive statements such as "I am intelligent," "I understand every question on the exam," and "I know the answers."

This time, Gabriel passed his National Counselor Examination!

 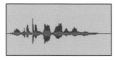

*When Gabriel previously said, "This test is silly" and "I don't think I am smart enough," the small energy resulted in his flunking his licensing examination.*

*Gabriel passed his examination when he stopped using negative phrases and started instead saying, "I understand every question on the exam" and "I know the answers—I am intelligent."*

## ANGEL WORDS TO
## SUPPORT YOUR DREAMS

Tamara Warden always dreamed of being a professional singer at weddings and nightclubs. When she was in school, she sang in choir and auditioned for solos. And then one of her best friends told her that her singing voice was "good, but not that good." Already a vulnerable teenager following her father's untimely death, Tamara's confidence was shattered. She gave up singing.

A few years later, Tamara got a deck of my *Magical Mermaids and Dolphins Oracle Cards*. Each time she'd give herself a reading, she would draw the "Music for Manifesting" card. But Tamara would always tell herself, "There's no way I can sing anymore," or "I can't sing; the cards must be wrong."

The Music oracle card came to Tamara for four years before she took action. She saw that a local nightclub was holding a karaoke competition and decided to give it a try. She sang her heart out, won fifth place out of 20 singers, and felt wonderful!

But the real prize was a heartfelt compliment from one of the other singers, who told Tamara that she had talent. The lady invited her to perform at a local music association, which led to Tamara gaining more confidence.

Now she's paid to sing at weddings, just like she'd always dreamed of! Tamara has even started her own karaoke business at the nightclub where she first returned to singing. She now encourages singers there to believe in themselves and to say, "I can do this!"

Tamara told me, "The power of positive thoughts has taught me to believe in myself and not to let negative thoughts or people crowd my mind. I am a good person, I do have talent, and I am worthwhile!" Tamara also shared that when she sings, she invites archangels Michael, Raphael, and Gabriel to be with her to keep her thoughts and music filled with positive blessings.

*When Tamara told herself, "I am not a good singer,"*
*she lost all confidence and gave up on her dream.*

*Tamara began singing professionally by affirming,*
*"I am a talented singer," which has high and supportive energy.*

One positive word can change your life for the better, as a woman named Jessica Nadeau discovered.

Jessica's life had been difficult for many years. She had one job after another, didn't seem able to stay in college, and at 36 years old was still living at home with her mother. When Jessica couldn't find a job after a year of looking, she became desperate for help.

That's when she began the study of spirituality and meditation. She soon noticed that she frequently heard and saw the word *benevolent,* although she didn't know its meaning. So Jessica consulted the dictionary, and she began to cry when she discovered its sweet definition: "marked by or disposed to doing good." She felt waves of relief and grace throughout her body as she reread it.

She began using the word as a mantra, and also focused upon seeing the benevolence within everyone and everything.

Jessica says: "I'm now happy to report I've been given a second chance to redeem the life I was meant to live, with a new job that is flexible enough to allow me to pursue a college degree in an area I'm truly passionate about! I'm filled with new and *benevolent* energy, and I know it will always be with me. This word has a positive effect on my life."

*Jessica said the very high-vibrational word* benevolent *(which means "kind, charitable, good") frequently, like a mantra. She credits this word with dramatically changing her life for the better.*

In a similar way, the word *grateful* made a big difference for a woman named Donna Domoleczny, who works the lunch shift as a server at a steakhouse. For a long time, the restaurant would be empty, since people seemed to want their steak as an evening, rather than an afternoon, meal. So Donna and her co-worker would moan and complain about their lack of income from customer tips.

Then Donna learned about the Law of Attraction, and she suggested to her co-worker that they could play a game as an experiment. She said, "Let's go around saying 'I am grateful' for every aspect of our work." So she and her co-worker started voicing their gratitude for the obvious factors, such as their jobs, the free food they got to eat, and their friendship.

Then they declared out loud their gratitude for rolling silverware in napkins, stacking serving plates, and every other task involved with their jobs. They weren't seriously feeling the gratitude, but just saying it jokingly. Nevertheless, the game made them laugh and shifted their moods upward.

The next day the restaurant was packed with customers, and they both made a lot of customer-tip money. Donna told me, "Gratitude really works! Sure, it's easier to complain, but once you start saying you're grateful, good things follow."

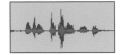

*When Donna and her co-worker continually complained, "Nobody eats here at lunch," their restaurant stayed empty. Notice in the graph that the middle part of the sentence shows high energy. That's where the phrase "eats here" was spoken, which is in itself a positive affirmation.*

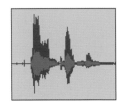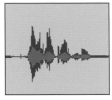

*The day after Donna and her co-worker began affirming, "I am grateful" and "We are grateful," the restaurant was packed with customers! Notice how the energy for "I am grateful" [graph on left] is stronger than "We are grateful" [graph on right].*

Your choice of words can make or break your business, finances, and career. That's why the old adage "You can't afford the luxury of a negative thought" is a time-honored truism. Positive words act as your business partner, mentor, and financial planner. They're an investment that costs nothing, yet which yields very high dividends.

Use only positive words to describe the global and local economy. Always affirm that your business, career, and finances are currently profitable and enjoyable. The use of positive words soon becomes a healthy, ingrained habit that ensures your financial health now and in the future.

In our next chapter, we'll look at how words act like healing angels.

33

# CHAPTER THREE

# ANGEL WORDS FOR HEALTH AND HEALING

*"Words are the physicians of a mind diseased."*

— AESCHYLUS

As the above quotation by the ancient Greek playwright implies, words can serve as healers. They can also be misused in the creation of illness.

When I worked in hospitals as a psychotherapist, I saw health-care professionals of two varieties:

1. The first (which thankfully constituted the majority) treated patients as people with complex feelings and individual situations.

2. The other type of health-care professional would refer to a patient by the person's diagnosis, such as saying, "The schizophrenic in Room 412." Their whole style objectified those they treated. In fact, I believe it taught patients to identify themselves as "a schizophrenic" instead of Judy, Bob, or Ralph. In such cases, medical and psychological diagnoses can act as self-fulfilling curses. This is where words can hurt.

Because I was raised in the healing religion Christian Science, my upbringing focused upon choosing words carefully . . . especially as they related to health. Instead of stating, "I have a cold," for example, I was taught to say something along the lines of "I seem to be having the experience of a cold," as a way of detaching from personally identifying with the illness.

Our beliefs held that we should avoid media reports (including commercials) about illnesses, as discussing or fearing sickness could lead to the development of those symptoms. I credit this training with my lifetime of good health.

Diagnostic labels can lead to self-fulfilling prophecies. So if you've received a particular diagnosis, it's important to detach from the words.

A man named Dominic used to tell himself and others, "I have been diagnosed with bipolar disorder." As part of that experience, he took psychiatric medications for most of a decade. Since he didn't want to be on drugs for his entire life, Dominic decided to harness the power of words to make healthy changes.

Now, he never uses the term *bipolar disorder* and only uses positive phrases when discussing his health. He frequently affirms, "I take excellent care of myself in all ways." Dominic worked with his doctor to become safely medication free. He says, "My mood and sleeping patterns are now very good. I've been inspired to take regular exercise and fresh air, quit smoking, and adopt a much more healthful lifestyle."

*When Dominic would constantly say, "I have been diagnosed with bipolar disorder," he manifested symptoms and the need for medication.*

*When Dominic stopped using the term* bipolar disorder, *and instead started saying, "I take excellent care of myself in all ways," he worked with his doctor to become safely medication free and adopted a healthful lifestyle.*

A woman named Anna Taylor had an experience similar to Dominic's. After being diagnosed with cerebral palsy as a child, she was widely labeled as "disabled." Even when she was very young, this term bothered her. It made her feel less than others, with limitations on what she could do.

As she grew up and became a professional singer, Anna discovered the power of sounds, tones, and words. This helped her understand why this particular word made her shudder. So now when others say that she's disabled, Anna declares, "I am very capable, thank you. Just not in all the ways you might be."

Instead of affirming that she has disabilities, Anna affirms that she has *abilities*. This has helped her overcome challenges, walk without a wheelchair, and record and release her singing

CD album. Anna told me, "I hope to share with others through my songs that whatever body we have, and whoever we are, we can all follow our dreams."

*When Anna would say, "I have disabilities,"*
*she'd feel less than others.*

*When Anna began affirming, "I have abilities," she was able*
*to walk without a wheelchair and follow her dreams of*
*becoming a professional singer with a CD album.*

Positive words are medicinal! When a woman named Krista Wiaz changed her vocabulary, her health improved. Diagnosed with fibromyalgia, Krista used to say, "This pain is never ending. I am tired of this pain. I hurt all over all the time," among other negative affirmations about her health.

One day Krista realized the negative impact that these pessimistic words were having upon her body. So now she says positive statements such as: "Well-being is my natural state of being. I am healthy, wealthy, and free. I have lots of energy to do the things I love."

Krista credits these positive phrases with the improvement in her life and health. She says, "Changing my thoughts from self-defeating ones to words of self-appreciation and self-love is healing my body. I am at a point that if I say 'tired,' I feel the weight come over me; and when I say I am healthy, wealthy, and free, the weight lifts from my shoulders."

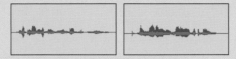

*When Krista complained, "This pain is never ending. I am tired of this pain. I hurt all over all the time," that's exactly what she experienced, along with a heavy weight on her shoulders.*

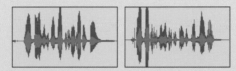

*The weight lifted from Krista's shoulders, her energy increased, and she began healing as she steadily affirmed, "Well-being is my natural state of being. I am healthy, wealthy, and free. I have lots of energy to do the things I love."*

As Krista's story illustrates, words can affect our energy levels faster than a cup of coffee.

A woman named Jessika Lazor used to say, "I'm so tired" and "I feel sick." After two years, doctors still couldn't find an organic cause for Jessika's exhaustion, headaches, and dizziness, so they gave her a diagnosis of chronic fatigue syndrome.

Finally, one day Jessika decided to try using positive affirmations. So she started saying to herself and others, "I have energy" and "I am healthy." Almost immediately, her energy level significantly increased and she felt better. She also felt energetic enough to move out of a toxic living situation, which contributed to her newfound health.

*Although doctors could find nothing wrong with her, Jessika continually said, "I'm so tired" and "I feel sick," and that's what she experienced.*

*When Jessika began affirming, "I have energy" and "I am healthy," her symptoms reversed and she became healthy and energetic.*

These stories are reminders to carefully choose how you describe yourself. Only use words portraying what you desire, such as *healthy, happy,* and *energetic.* As the Angel Words graphs show, negative health descriptions are low-energy, leading to low-energy symptoms. Fortunately, though, every negative word has a positive antonym that can heal your life and boost your self-esteem, as we'll explore in the next chapter.

# CHAPTER FOUR

# LIFE-AFFIRMING CLICHÉS AND EXPRESSIONS

*"Kind words can be short and easy to speak,
but their echoes are truly endless."*

— MOTHER TERESA

I love birds. I feed the wild ones in my yard, and even carry a little bag of birdseed in my car to feed sparrows who land nearby in parking lots. So when someone recently uttered the cliché "Kill two birds with one stone," I naturally cringed.

Then I spoke up. With a smile, I gently suggested a more life-affirming alternative: "How about if we 'Feed two birds with one handful of bird food'?"

The other person and I both laughed and acknowledged the truth: it's so important to watch all the words we speak, think, or write . . . including time-honored clichés.

Growing up, Esther Hill used to hear her father say, "Life is not a bowl of cherries." Like any impressionable young child would do, she believed her dad's words, so as an adult, she used the same expression frequently. Her life was difficult, but she accepted that this was just the way it was supposed to be.

Then Esther met people who taught her that you could control your life with the use of positive affirmations. So she started to say, "Life *is* a bowl of cherries," and her life completely turned around!

Esther says: "Now I have a wonderful life, I'm learning new things every day, and life is exciting! I can do so much and be whomever I want to be. I have a gorgeous partner, live in a fantastic house, and own my own business; and I help other people get into a higher vibration in life. Life is so, *so* a bowl of cherries!"

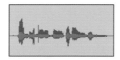

*Esther learned to say, "Life is not a bowl of cherries" from her father, which led to her belief that life was supposed to be difficult.*

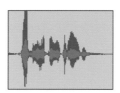

*When Esther turned the cliché into a positive "Life* is *a bowl of cherries!" her life became happier and filled up with exciting new opportunities.*

## Peaceful Clichés

Clichés such as Esther's seem harmless enough, until you realize that saying them repeatedly carves out your reality. I worked with several Angel Therapists® to create peaceful alternatives to negative clichés, and here's the list we created. Notice the low vibrations on the graphs of the old sayings and the high vibrations on new ones:

### Old Cliché

### New Cliché

Kill two birds with one stone.

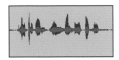

Feed two birds with one handful of bird food.

It's my slavings account.

It's my blessings account—there is always money in it.

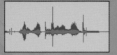

That's a real pain (in the neck)!

That's a bit of a challenge!

I nearly had a heart attack!

It really made me jump.

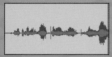

I'm between a rock
and a hard place.

I move through life
with ease and grace.

There's more than one way
to skin a cat.

The world is full of infinite
possibility. *Or:* There is more than
one way to kiss and pet a cat.

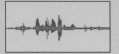

Awfully nice of her/him.

Awesome of her/him!

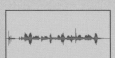

"Close" only counts in horseshoes, hand grenades, and atomic bombs.

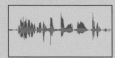

"Close" also counts in love, family, and friendships.

I am open to criticism.

I am open to positive feedback!

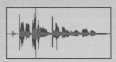

It's like stealing candy from a baby.

The sweetness in life *is* plentiful for all of our inner child's desires!

He's a few bricks short of
a full load.

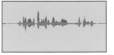

His possibilities are unlimited and
overflowing with complete genius.

I had a hell of a good time.

I had a *heaven* of a good time.

I've been dying for this moment.

I've been *living* for this moment.

Damned if you do,
damned if you don't.

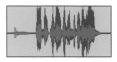

Blessed if you do,
blessed if you don't,
blessed no matter what!

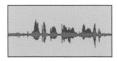

No good deed goes unpunished.

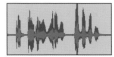

Good deeds are rewarding
on every level.

I'm as serious as a heart attack.

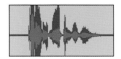

This is my truth.

I'm just telling you how it is.

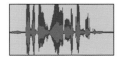

Everybody's reality is different.

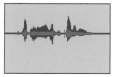

Luxury is an enemy.

Luxury is like our soul-mate lover!

This tastes like sh**.

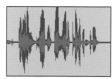

This has a flavor I'm not accustomed to.

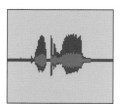

Break a leg!

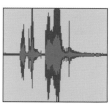

You can do it.
*Or:* May the Force be with you.

One shot, one kill!

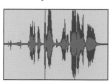

First attempt, success!

A cat in hell's chance.

Every chance under the sun.

I am sweating like a pig.

My body is releasing toxins and cleansing itself.

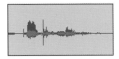

I don't give a f***.

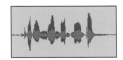

It's no fluff off my duck!

All's fair in love and war.

Love is real.

Money doesn't grow on trees.

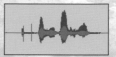

We live in a rich and abundant universe.

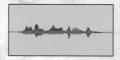

*K.I.S.S.* (Keep It Simple, Stupid.)

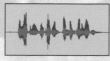

Keep It Simple, Sweetie.

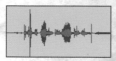

It's not brain surgery.

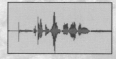

It is easy compared to most things.

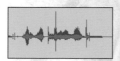

What a pain in the neck.

It's a real learning experience.

Everything I love is illegal, immoral, or fattening.

Life is great!

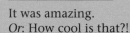

I can't believe that.
*Or:* It was unbelievable.

It was amazing.
*Or*: How cool is that?!

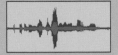

Children should be
seen and not heard.

Children should be seen
and heard loud and clear!

There's no end in sight.

Wonderful changes happen
all the time!

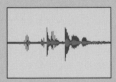

I could've killed him.

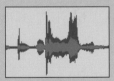

I could've hugged him.

If it was a snake,
it would have bitten you!

If it was my dog, it would
have licked you!

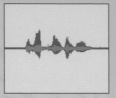

My heart bleeds for you.

My heart sings for you.

Drop-dead gorgeous!

Gorgeous!

I'm sick and tired of this.

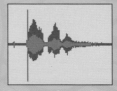

I am ready to change this.

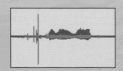

Get over it.

Release it.

Life's a bitch and
then you die.

Killing time.

Life is hard.

Lesser of two evils.

Life's a blessing if you try. *Or:*
Life's a blessing, then you fly!

Enjoying life.

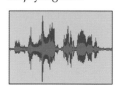

Life is *full* of opportunities!

The best opportunity that
presents itself.

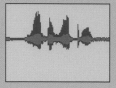

My heart goes out to you.

What can I do to support you?

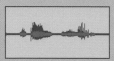

No pain no gain.

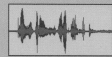

Positive change is worth the effort.

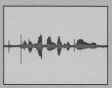

The suspense is killing me.

I am excited to find out.

That is no skin off my back.

It's easy!

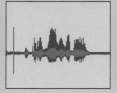

It's been a heck of a day.

It's been a heaven of a day!

With gratitude to our Angel Therapist team who helped to produce this list, including: Ros Booth, Anna Taylor, Hope Cramer, Sue Tanida, Tatiela Laake, Pat Schiavo, Tony Costa, April P. Eriel, Angela Hartfield, Clare Douglas, Corrinne White, Arlette Bellio, Mary Morningstar Collins, Brigitte Parvin, Janet Bowden, Satoshi Morikawa, David Alden, Melanie Jacob, Erica Longdon, Wendy Eidman, Patrick Richardson, Julie Ann Moylan, Isabella Wesoly, Kristi Vaughn, Megan Anne Gay, Paula Masterman, Claire Jennings, Kate Whorlow, Sandra Allagapen, Keri Martin, Heidi Boucher, Chantal Provost, Kristi Vaughn, Polly Ford, Lisette-Anne Volker, Catherine McMahon, Timothy Ellis, and Lori R. Leach.

According to Webster's dictionary, *cliché* is a French word that was originally jargon used by printers. The past participle of the verb *clicher,* it describes the process of duplicating words with printing presses. So the basis of the word is imitation or duplication.

Today, *cliché* is a noun used to describe trite expressions, commonplace idioms, and familiar phrases. While it's easy to parrot clichés and say them mindlessly, you must remember that each phrase acts the same as if you were ordering from a menu at a restaurant. Every time you say it, you're telling the universe what you desire. And like a waiter at a restaurant, the universe will simply deliver whatever you order. The waiter isn't going to argue, "Hey, wait—that item isn't good for your health!" He's simply going to bring you what you asked for.

So let's continue our exploration of ways to shift our lives in even more positive directions through being consciously aware of the words we choose and use. Our next chapter will examine how words can be angels that heal us.

# CHAPTER FIVE

# WORDS CAN HEAL YOUR LIFE

*"Words form the thread on which
we string our experiences."*

— ALDOUS HUXLEY

You've seen the energy of words in the stories and graphs within this book. You can immediately change any part of your life just by using higher-vibrating words. In this chapter, you'll meet people who have become more positive simply by adding optimistic words and terms into their vocabularies. Like taking vitamins or eating organic salads, positive statements are simple yet powerful tools that boost happiness, peace, and self-esteem.

Emma Horton works with children at an outdoor-activity center. As the children attempt to scale the vertical climbing wall,

she hears them complain, "I can't!" So Emma coaches each child to instead use the affirmation "I can do it!" As the kids climb higher on the wall, she helps them to replace each "can't" with "can" until they reach the top. The children are always elated that they did it! This gives them the confidence to tackle other challenges.

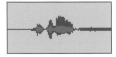

*When children say "I can't," they're unable to scale the vertical climbing wall at Emma's outdoor-activity center.*

*As Emma encourages kids to say "I can do it!" they're able to climb to the top of the wall.*

Just as they did for the children on Emma's climbing wall, words can act like motivational coaches that help you do your best. Jessika Lazor, whom you met earlier, experienced a profound shift when she stopped using negative, apologetic terms such as "I'm sorry" or "I feel bad." She realized that these two phrases were creating guilt instead of bringing healing energy to her and others. So now she says, "I forgive myself" whenever she thinks she made a mistake. Jessika told me, "Saying 'I forgive myself' has been one of the most life-changing things I've ever done."

With the burden of guilt lessened, Jessika now feels much better about herself, and she has stopped compulsively apologizing for things she had nothing to do with. She says, "I can now enjoy just being myself!"

*When Jessika would compulsively apologize for things, she'd say,*
*"I feel bad" and "I am sorry," which made her feel worse about herself.*

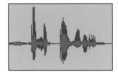

*Jessika feels much better about herself now that she says,*
*"I forgive myself" whenever she believes she has made a mistake.*

## GOOD LUCK!

The old adages "There's no such thing as luck" and "You make your own luck" have kernels of truth to them, as a woman named Lucia Kosinova has noted.

Lucia constantly said, "For sure, with my bad luck, something will go wrong" . . . and of course, it always did. After becoming more spiritually aware of the way in which energy affects us, Lucia wanted to live a more positive and empowered life.

So she started saying, "I am loved. I am guided and protected, and this situation will resolve," whenever she met with challenging circumstances. Since that time, Lucia's life has dramatically transformed, and she is helping other people lead positive lives.

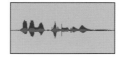

*Lucia used to say, "With my bad luck, something will go wrong,"
and that's exactly what she experienced.*

*When Lucia decided to live a more empowered life,
she stopped talking about bad luck and instead started saying,
"I am loved. I am guided and protected, and this situation
will resolve," whenever she was presented with a challenge.
The positive energy of this statement brings wonderful results.*

## ANGEL WORDS AND RELATIONSHIPS

Every relationship has a spiritual purpose that helps us grow
and become stronger. Sometimes, our most challenging relationships bring the greatest personal blessings. From them we learn
about forgiveness, patience, and other virtues.

Since communication is the crux of most relationships, the words you say to others can impact the quality of your interactions. Use kind and loving words and you'll have kind and loving personal connections. Use harsh or unloving words and your relationships will follow suit.

Probably the most important words are the ones that we speak to ourselves. These words can affect how we feel about and view ourselves, which in turn will affect our relationships with other people.

For example, a woman named Fairouz Saouli rarely saw her father growing up. She developed a belief that he didn't love her and that she didn't deserve his affection. This belief grew as Fairouz got older, resulting in her conviction that she didn't deserve any love from a man. Consequently, her romantic relationships were empty and dissatisfying as she chose unloving, undemonstrative men.

This all changed when Fairouz learned about the Law of Attraction at a spiritual class. She found out about positive affirmations, which caused her to stop saying her previous affirmation, "I don't deserve love," and to instead affirm repeatedly, "I deserve to receive love."

Soon after she started stating these positive words, Fairouz increased her amount of contact with her father. She also went to see him, which helped her make peace with him and find relief. Fairouz was happy as she sat on the airplane waiting for the other passengers to board on her flight home from her visit with her father. Just then a man got on the plane, and she had the spontaneous thought: *I'm going to marry him one day.* Sure enough, the man sat next to Fairouz, and the two had wonderful conversations on the long flight from Europe to Canada.

Over the course of the next several months, they e-mailed, called, and visited one another. Today, they live happily together, and Fairouz finally feels loved. She says, "All this

happened because I changed my thinking. This was the best thing I could have done for myself."

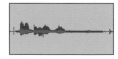

*Fairouz constantly told herself, "I don't deserve love," and as a result, had continued difficulty in her relationships.*

*When Fairouz began affirming, "I deserve to receive love," she immediately met and fell in love with a wonderful man.*

As Fairouz's story demonstrates, "self-talk" (the words you say to yourself) can determine the course of your relationships. If you think negative words and phrases, this pushes people away. The low energy they contain, as demonstrated in the graphs, isn't at all attractive. Yet when you change to a more positive vocabulary, the energy becomes greater and more inviting.

Similar to that of Fairouz, Val Tobin's negative self-talk interfered with her desire for warm, loving relationships. Each time

Val would meet someone new, she'd think, *This person doesn't like me.* Since childhood, she'd assumed that others would dislike and reject her. This resulted in her acting aloof and cold to people, which ensured that they wouldn't warm up to her.

It took a real conscious effort, but Val finally turned around her self-talk and made it positive. She began to tell herself, "They'll like me when they get to know me. I like them, too." Val says that these psitive thoughts were akin to opening a window and letting in fresh air. She found herself spontaneously smiling and talking more, because she no longer assumed that people would reject her.

Val says, "Now I feel more connected to people. I know that we're all one, and that I'm not a terrible person who's unworthy of affection. I know I am lovable!"

*Val habitually thought,* They don't like me, *whenever she met someone new, which made her relationships strained and cold.*

*Val began having healthy relationships with herself and others when she started affirming, "They'll like me when they get to know me. I like them, too."*

## CURSE WORDS

In addition to the words we think, the ones we say aloud have a profound effect on us. Curse words are like missiles that explode negative energy upon impact. While swearing can temporarily

alleviate fear or anger for the person speaking, the words contaminate everyone within earshot. And as a woman named Sharon discovered, their negative energies boomerang back to the one who utters them.

Sharon used to use the "f" word a lot. Most of the time, she said it under her breath so that it was only audible to her. The word was like a secret rebel tactic, in which she'd vocalize her displeasure without upsetting anyone . . . well, anyone but *herself,* that is.

As Sharon focused upon her spiritual path, she became more sensitive to energy. And she noticed that whenever she said the "f" word, she'd feel drained. After this observation, Sharon began to mentally stop herself from using it.

Whenever she was tempted to curse, Sharon would pause and say "Bless you" instead. This helped her blood pressure drop and her moods stabilize.

*When Sharon was angry, she'd say the "f" word
and her blood pressure would increase.*

*Now Sharon says "Bless you" instead, and her blood pressure has decreased.*

## BENDING TIME WITH WORDS

By now, these stories and graphs probably have shown you how to improve your life by altering what you say, think, and write. Positive words can aid your career and finances, health, self-esteem, and relationships. In fact, they're so powerful and magical that they can help you to seemingly defy physical laws, such as those relating to time.

Many people have used positive affirmations about time in order to "bend" it. When I appear to be running late, I calmly state, "I arrive at the perfect time," and I always do. These words help me encounter green stoplights and flowing traffic. Sometimes they will help me arrive with illogical swiftness—without speeding. Other times, I'll arrive a bit late and the people I'm meeting will be late, too. The words allow me to be calm so that I'm fresh and relaxed when I get to my destination.

Here's the graph for this magical phrase that will ensure your punctuality from now on:

*Affirming the high-energy statement "I arrive at the perfect time" will keep you calm, cool, and punctual.*

Livia Maris Jepsen, whom you met in an earlier chapter, used a similar affirmation about time recently, with beautiful results. She'd left home later than expected to drive to the airport. Logically speaking, she shouldn't have been able to make her flight, but Livia knows the power of words, so she called upon the angels and said, "Please help me get to the gate with plenty of time to spare!"

When Livia arrived at the airport, the check-in line was huge, but she had faith that her prayer would be answered. The line moved quickly, and she arrived at the boarding gate 30 minutes prior to takeoff. Just as Livia was about to thank the angels

for her "plenty of time to spare," an agent announced that the plane would be delayed another 30 minutes. So Livia's positive words, her prayers, and the angels had delivered her to the airport gate a full hour ahead of departure time!

And because Livia kept the faith while driving to the airport and waiting in line, she enjoyed stress-free air travel.

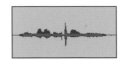

*Saying "There's never enough time" creates stress,
and the self-fulfilling prophecy of being chronically late.*

*Livia's prayer and affirmation on the way to the airport was
to reach her gate with "plenty of time to spare," and she miraculously
arrived an hour before her flight's departure.*

Words are the building blocks that create the foundation for your happiness . . . or misery. Your choice. The great news is that you have complete control over which words you choose to think, say, and write.

If you're in a situation or relationship where negative words are being used, you can shield yourself by mentally saying, *That may be true for you, but it's not true for me,* and praying for protection. With prayer, guided action, and uplifting words, you can rebuild your life so that you're only surrounded by supportive people. All you have to do is repeatedly say things like "Everyone in my life is positive and speaks positively," and by virtue of the Law of Attraction, it must occur.

In the next chapter, we'll look at graphs of various words so that you can continue to see the energy of positive and negative examples. It might even be helpful to show these graphs to the people you live and work with as a way of inspiring others to speak positively.

Chapter Six

# CHAPTER SIX

# POSITIVE, HIGH-ENERGY WORDS

*"Man's word is God in man."*

— ALFRED, LORD TENNYSON

The next few chapters show the graphs of positive and negative words to demonstrate the energy within them. This chapter will focus upon positive words. We realize that a word can have a positive meaning to one person and a negative one to another, based upon personal experiences with the word, the individual's mood at the time, and other factors. Still, our experiments with reading words aloud and studying their subsequent graphs (such as the experiment with saying "love" and "hate" with the same four emotions, as outlined in the Introduction) show that they carry an innate essence of either positive or negative energy.

This is a great list of words to sprinkle throughout your speech . . . or—better yet—to fill up your vocabulary! Notice the beautiful, expansive energy of each positive word, extending the light and love contained within its meaning. These words are all about sharing and loving.

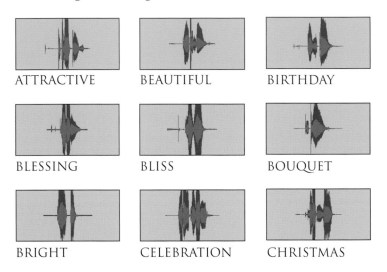

ATTRACTIVE  BEAUTIFUL  BIRTHDAY

BLESSING  BLISS  BOUQUET

BRIGHT  CELEBRATION  CHRISTMAS

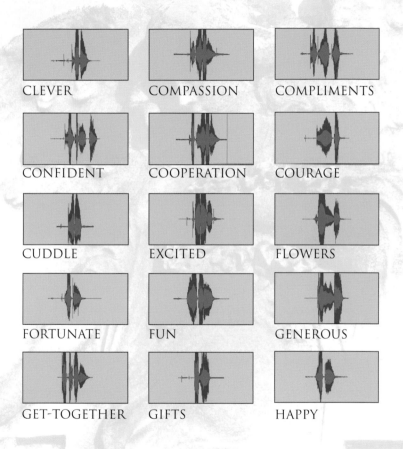

CLEVER

COMPASSION

COMPLIMENTS

CONFIDENT

COOPERATION

COURAGE

CUDDLE

EXCITED

FLOWERS

FORTUNATE

FUN

GENEROUS

GET-TOGETHER

GIFTS

HAPPY

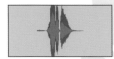

HEALTHY

HILARIOUS

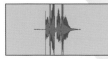

HOLIDAY

HUG

INTEGRITY

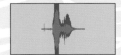

JOY

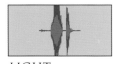

KISSES

LAUGHTER

LIGHT

LOVE

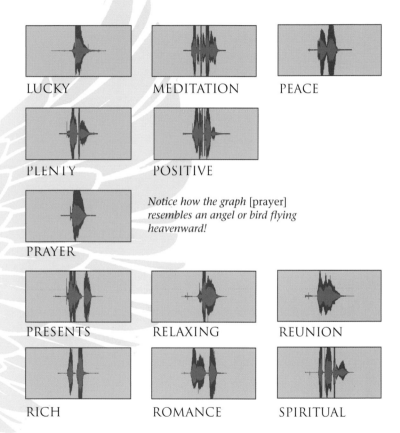

LUCKY

MEDITATION

PEACE

PLENTY

POSITIVE

PRAYER

*Notice how the graph [prayer] resembles an angel or bird flying heavenward!*

PRESENTS

RELAXING

REUNION

RICH

ROMANCE

SPIRITUAL

STRENGTH

TRUST

VACATION

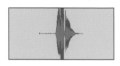

WISDOM

Positive words are beautiful feeling, sounding, and looking. Their expansive energies elevate and inspire you like angels lifting you skyward. Once you become attuned to the feelings and sounds of positive, high-vibrational words, the negative ones become distasteful.

In the next chapter, we'll look at the energies of common negative words to show the graphs of low-vibrational energies.

# CHAPTER SEVEN

# NEGATIVE, LOW-ENERGY WORDS

*"Colors fade, temples crumble, empires fall,*
*but wise words endure."*

— EDWARD THORNDIKE

This wasn't a fun chapter to create and probably won't be the most pleasant one to read in this book; however, we feel it's important to showcase the graphs of negative words in a separate place. These pages may feel unpleasant or heavy to those who are sensitive to energies. For this we apologize in advance. Please know that you can clear the energy of negativity with positive affirmations. The light always shines away darkness. (In the Afterword of this book, we also include some methods for shielding yourself from, and clearing, negativity.)

The value of this chapter lies in its contrast to the previous one. Notice how small, shrunken, and constricted the graphs that follow are. They represent the low energy of the fear behind negativity, the belief in lack and limitation, and the conviction that selfishness is necessary for survival. These are old energies that are, fortunately, on their way out of civilization as we collectively choose to focus upon cooperation, love, and manifestation.

ACCIDENT

ADDICTION

ANGER

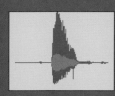

ANXIETY

AWFUL

*Notice the large spike on this graph* [awful], *which we believe stems from the "Aw" prefix. Ahh is one of the Divine sounds found within most names for the Creator (for example,* God, Allah, Father, Buddha, Omni, Shiva, *and the like).*

BAD

BILLS

CANCER

CIGARETTES

*Hey, what can I say? I'm an ex-smoker, so I think this word* [cigarettes] *belongs in this chapter.*

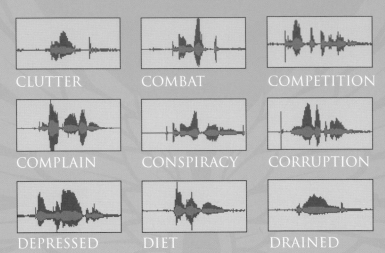

CLUTTER COMBAT COMPETITION

COMPLAIN CONSPIRACY CORRUPTION

DEPRESSED DIET DRAINED

*Notice that this is a larger graph [drugs], indicating that the word can be neutral or positive. Contrast this with the word* addiction, *which yields a small graph and has entirely negative connotations.*

DRUGS

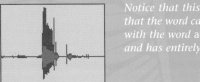

EXHAUSTED FAILURE

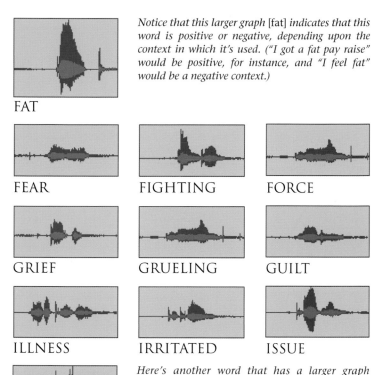

FAT

*Notice that this larger graph [fat] indicates that this word is positive or negative, depending upon the context in which it's used. ("I got a fat pay raise" would be positive, for instance, and "I feel fat" would be a negative context.)*

FEAR

FIGHTING

FORCE

GRIEF

GRUELING

GUILT

ILLNESS

IRRITATED

ISSUE

JUNK

*Here's another word that has a larger graph [junk], which indicates that it's either positive or negative depending upon its context. (For example, "This car is junk" would be negative, and "I found lots of good junk at the garage sale" would be positive.)*

NEGATIVE

OVERDUE

PAIN

PESTICIDE

*This graph [pesticide] is a good case for only eating organic foods and using organic personal products. Who would want to ingest negative energy in their foods or skin lotions?*

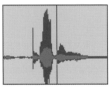

PLAGUING

*The large size of this graph [plaguing] shows that this word can have negative or positive energies, depending on the context. (That is, "My desire for chocolate has been plaguing me!" would be more positive, while any sentence in which something unpleasant is "plaguing" you would be negative.)*

POISON

*This is always a negative word [poison], unless you're a fan of the '80s big-hair rock band with this name.*

POLITICIAN

*From the size of the graph, this is a negative word [politician] in any context.*

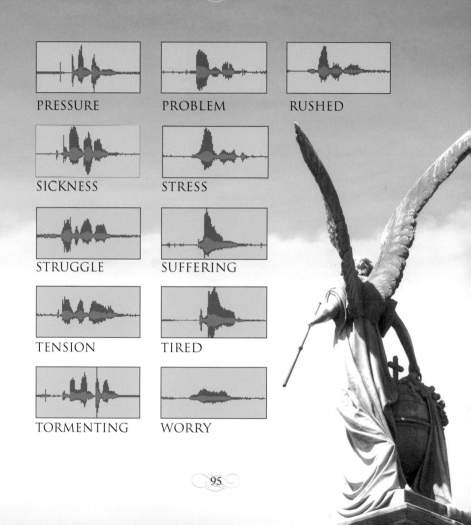

PRESSURE

PROBLEM

RUSHED

SICKNESS

STRESS

STRUGGLE

SUFFERING

TENSION

TIRED

TORMENTING

WORRY

Our intention with this chapter is to let you see how low the energy is within negative words. We hope these graphs will inspire you to choose high-energy, positive ones.

Any complaint or worry can be recast from a negative into a positive. For instance, the fear "I am afraid of being alone" can be rewritten into an encouraging affirmation: "I love being with other people." The latter statement has a higher vibration and will likely attract wonderful relationships.

In the next chapter, you'll see a comparison of high- and low-vibrating words side by side to clearly illustrate the differences.

# CHAPTER EIGHT

# A COMPARISON OF HIGH- AND LOW- ENERGY WORDS

*"If you wish to know the mind of a man, listen to his words."*
— JOHANN WOLFGANG VON GOETHE

In this chapter, Grant has recorded pairs of antonyms so that we can see the energy graphs of positive and negative words side by side. This comparison of high- and low-energy utterances is a dramatic illustration of the differences between words.

In my book *Divine Magic,* I discuss the Hermetic teachings, revealing how opposites are viewed as two ends of the same pole. For example, hot and cold are on either end of the spectrum called "temperature." So the two are related.

In the same way, antonyms share similar root topics. As mentioned earlier, there's always a positive and a negative way to express the same sentiment. It's just that positive words make the sentiment so much more palatable and high-vibrational.

Some people purposely use fear-based speech to engender fear or guilt as a way of manipulating others or justifying their actions. As you become sensitive to the differences between high- and low-energy words, you're more likely to recognize, resist, and avoid such tactics. Through the Law of Attraction, the more you use high-energy, positive words, the more you'll *attract* high-energy, positive relationships and situations.

## Positive-to-Negative Antonyms

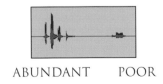

ABUNDANT        POOR

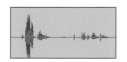

ACCEPTING    JUDGMENTAL

ADMIRATION    JEALOUSY

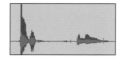

ASK    DEMAND

BELOVED    LONELY

BLISS    ANGER

BUILD    DESTROY

CAREFUL    CARELESS

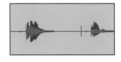

CLEAN    DIRTY

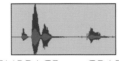

EMBRACE    GRAB

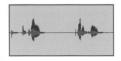

EMPLOYED    UNEMPLOYED

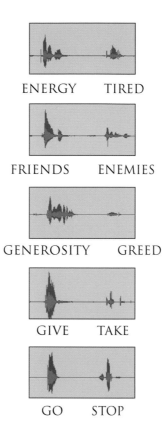

ENERGY        TIRED

FRIENDS        ENEMIES

GENEROSITY        GREED

GIVE        TAKE

GO        STOP

# ANGEL WORDS

GOOD     BAD

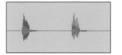

HAPPY     SAD

HEALTH     ILLNESS

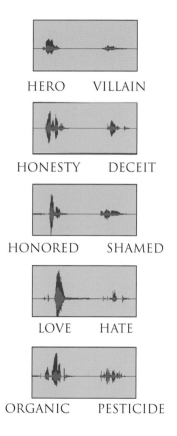

HERO     VILLAIN

HONESTY     DECEIT

HONORED     SHAMED

LOVE     HATE

ORGANIC     PESTICIDE

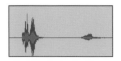

PEACE     WAR

POSITIVE     NEGATIVE

PROTECT     POSSESS

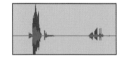

QUIET     SHUT UP

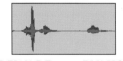

REWARD     PUNISH

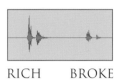

RICH        BROKE

SAVINGS      DEBT

SECURE      FEAR

SHARING     SELFISH

SOLAR       COAL

SOLUTION     PROBLEM

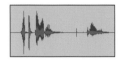

STABILITY     DRAMA

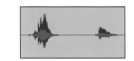

THOUGHTFUL     RUDE

WARM     FREEZING

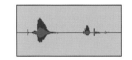

WHOLE     BROKEN

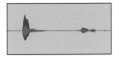

WIN     LOSE

Positive words, with their higher vibrations, are actually energizing to say, write, and think! To elevate your energy, make sure to use as many as possible throughout the day.

Higher energy is correlated with faster manifestations of your intentions and goals. It gives spark and oomph to all that you do. It also effectively gives you more usable time during each day, since you have more drive to get more accomplished.

Positive words are readily available and free of charge. It just makes *sense* to use them!

# AFTERWORD

*"Words are the voice of the heart."*
— Confucius

The spiritual text *A Course in Miracles* says that the ego (the fear-based part of your mind) wants to make spirituality complicated, exotic, and always slightly out of reach. The truth of attaining peace is actually simple, though, says the *Course*. It's a matter of deciding to focus upon love instead of fear. It's a decision based upon your willingness to allow love into your life.

Part of this decision entails changing your thoughts to become more positive. So what *are* thoughts? Well, they include the words you tell yourself and what you think when you see or hear someone or encounter some situation. It really is that simple.

Yet, as I mentioned, our lower-self egos want to make spirituality complicated and unattainable. The ego wants us to suffer and climb mountains to reach enlightenment, when really it's a matter of making our vocabulary more positive, as Monique Jean discovered.

Although Monique had studied metaphysics for more than a decade, she continued to tell herself that she wasn't knowledgeable enough, wasn't progressing fast enough, wasn't spiritual enough, wasn't clairvoyant enough, and so forth. When she realized that she was blocking herself with negative self-talk, she made a conscious decision to speak with more positive words.

So she started saying, "I am clairvoyant. I am knowledgeable. I am talented." She immediately began to feel fearless, peaceful, and confident that she could do whatever she intended. Monique was empowered by these positive words! Now she's enjoying a new career and is writing, healing, and teaching. Ideas, guidance, and inspiration come to her much more easily and quickly now, and her manifestations appear more rapidly . . . all thanks to her decision to use positive words!

*When Monique affirmed that she wasn't enough by saying "I'm not clairvoyant enough" and "I don't know enough about spirituality," she experienced blocks.*

 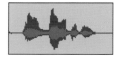

*Monique's decision to speak about herself in positive terms opened many doors of opportunity and joy for her. Her positive affirmations are "I am clairvoyant," "I am knowledgeable," and "I am talented."*

## CANCEL, CLEAR, DELETE

My friends, family, and I all support each other in our collective decision to use positive words. We know that speaking negatively can result in negative experiences. Yet even the most conscientious person slips up occasionally. To undo the effects of a negative word or phrase, you can say or think, "Cancel, clear, delete," just like rebooting a computer.

We do this for each other when one of us isn't consciously aware of saying a negative affirmation. The same with complaints: If someone in our group says something like "I always attract needy people," the rest of us will say: "In the past!" We help each other realize that a pattern in the past doesn't have to continue in the present or future. Changing the way in which we describe our patterns is empowering!

We also use the "sorceress sweep" (for females) or "sorcerer sweep" (for males) to clear away the energy of negative words. It simply means waving your hand as if you're shooing something away.

I also love Louise L. Hay's affirmation "That may be true for you, but it's not true for me," which she silently thinks when she encounters a person speaking negatively. This has a shielding and "undoing" effect.

Speaking of shielding, if you're in a situation with harsh energy (such as competitiveness or arguing), remember to call upon Archangel Michael to surround you with purple light. Only love can permeate this protective light.

Hopefully, you'll empower yourself to avoid those who chronically speak negatively. You don't need to wallow in toxic energies! Call upon your God, your higher self, and the angels for protection and guidance to rearrange your life so that you're sur-rounded by the gentlest and highest of energies. You can do this!

## POSITIVE WORDS FOR THE EARTH

As you've seen in this book, your choice of words can make a huge difference in your life. Positive words can also help others . . . and the entire world!

Please, when describing the world, remember to use posi-tive words. Speak in terms of what you desire—not about fears, doom, or gloom. The earth, like people, responds to energies. You elevate it with positive words.

For example, saying something fear based like "Humans have ruined the earth's environment" has low energy, as this graph illustrates:

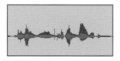

*This is a graph of the negative affirmation*
*"Humans have ruined the earth's environment," showing its low energy.*

Instead, affirm your desire for the earth, such as "Our environment is healthy," shown in this graph:

*The positive affirmation "Our environment is healthy"*
*gifts the earth with high energy.*

Of course, you'll want to back up your positive affirmations by taking eco-friendly action such as recycling and using environmentally safe cleaning supplies.

The same thing applies with statements about the economy. Here's how the negative affirmation "We're in a recession" looks on an energy graph:

*Saying "We're in a recession" releases low energy into the world*
*and negatively affects your personal "economy," too.*

Another phrase that adversely impacts financial flow is: "In this bad economy . . ." I've heard many business owners start sentences with this phrase, which is low-energy, as this graph illustrates:

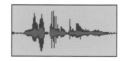

*Beginning sentences with the phrase "In this bad economy . . ."*
*can block your personal financial flow.*

You can stimulate your own personal economy, as well as help others, by affirming, "There is plenty of abundance for everyone," which shows high energy on this graph:

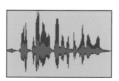

*Affirming "There is plenty of abundance for everyone"*
*is a high-energy way to fuel your economy.*

Another positive affirmation is "The economy is healthy here," which also has high energy and magnetism, as this graph illustrates:

*Saying "The economy is healthy here"*
*has high energy that attracts abundance.*

In the same way, beware of doom-and-gloom statements about the world ending. Such statements are low-energy, as this graph shows:

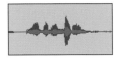

*Doom-and-gloom statements such as*
*"The world will end soon" aren't helpful to you or the planet.*

To *really* help yourself and the planet, use positive words such as this high-energy affirmation: "Our planet is an eternal gift from God." This declaration is healing, helpful, and spiritually true.

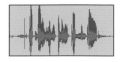

*Saying, writing, or thinking, "Our planet is an eternal gift from God"
sends high, positive energy out into the world.*

Many people ask me what they can do to help themselves and the planet, and with positive words, you've got the ultimate tool right on the tip of your tongue. Together, we can all speak empowering and healing words that support us on our collective mission for a peaceful, healthy planet with abundance and love for everyone.

It's all about the highest energy of all . . . *love.*

# BIBLIOGRAPHY

Chladni, E. Discoveries in the Theory of Sound *(Entdeckungen Uber Die Theorie Des Klanges)*, 1787. 2009: Kessinger Publishing.

Deeprose, C., et al. Unconscious learning during surgery with propofol anaesthesia. British Journal of Anaesthesia, 2004; Vol. 92, No. 2: 171–7.

Handwerker, W. Penn. Childhood Origins of Depression. Journal of Women's Health, 1999; Vol. 8, No. 1.

Hazlett, E. A. Exaggerated affect-modulated startle during unpleasant stimuli in borderline personality disorder. Biol Psychiatry, 2007 Aug 1; 62(3): 250–5.

Miyake, Y., et al. Neural processing of negative word stimuli concerning body image in patients with eating disorders: an fMRI study. Neuroimage, 2010 April 15; 50(3): 1333–9.

Nasrallah, M.; Carmel, D.; Lavie, N. Murder, she wrote: Enhanced sensitivity to negative word valence. Emotion, Oct 2009; 9(5): 609–618.

Richter, M.; Eck, J.; Straube, T.; Miltner, W. H. R.; Weiss, T. Do words hurt? Brain activation during explicit and implicit processing of pain words. Pain, 2010; 148(2): 198 205.

Shirao, N., et al. Gender differences in brain activity toward unpleasant linguistic stimuli concerning interpersonal relationships: an fMRI study. European Archives of Psychiatry and Clinical Neuroscience, 2005; Vol. 255, No. 5.

Shirao, N., et al. Temporomesial activation in young females associated with unpleasant words concerning body image. Neuropsychobiology, 2003; 48: 136–142.

Wang, F., et al. Negative words on surgical wards result in therapeutic failure of patient-controlled analgesia and further release of cortisol after abdominal surgeries. Minerva Anestesiol, 2008 Jul–Aug; 74(7–8): 353–65.

# ABOUT THE AUTHORS

**Doreen Virtue** holds B.A. and M.A. degrees in counseling psychology from Chapman University, a Ph.D. in counseling psychology from California Coast University, and an associate's degree from Antelope Valley College. She is a lifelong clairvoyant who works with the angelic realm.

Doreen has previously written about the power of words in *Divine Magic: The Seven Sacred Secrets of Manifestation.* She's also the best-selling author of *How to Hear Your Angels, Messages from*

*Your Angels, Archangels & Ascended Masters,* and *Solomon's Angels;* as well as the *Archangel Oracle Cards,* among other works. Her products are available in most languages worldwide.

Doreen has appeared on *Oprah,* CNN, *The View,* and other television and radio programs. She writes regular columns for *Woman's World, Spheres,* and *Spirit & Destiny* magazines. For more information on Doreen and the workshops she presents, please visit: **www.AngelTherapy.com**.

You can listen to Doreen's live weekly radio show, and call her for a reading, by visiting **HayHouseRadio.com**®.

**Grant Virtue** is Doreen's son, a fifth-generation metaphysician, and the co-author of the *Angel Blessings Candle Kit*. Grant has studied candle magic and music theory extensively throughout his life. In addition to writing books, he is the Education Administrator for Angel University, and he plays and records meditation music.

For more information about Grant, please visit: **www.Angel University.com**.

# Hay House Titles of Related Interest

*YOU CAN HEAL YOUR LIFE, the movie,* starring Louise L. Hay & Friends
(available as a 1-DVD program and an expanded 2-DVD set)
Watch the trailer at: **www.LouiseHayMovie.com**

*THE SHIFT, the movie,*
starring Dr. Wayne W. Dyer
(available as a 1-DVD program and an expanded 2-DVD set)
Watch the trailer at: **www.DyerMovie.com**

*CREATING INNER HARMONY: Using Your Voice and Music to Heal,*
by Don Campbell (book-with-CD)

*THE DIVINE NAME: The Sound That Can Change the World,*
by Jonathan Goldman (book-with-CD)

*EXPERIENCE YOUR GOOD NOW!: Learning to Use Affirmations,*
by Louise L. Hay (book-with-CD)

*MESSAGES FROM WATER AND THE UNIVERSE,*
by Masaru Emoto

*ORBS: Their Mission & Messages of Hope,*
by Klaus Heinemann, Ph.D., and Gundi Heinemann

*SAVED BY A POEM: The Transformative Power of Words,*
by Kim Rosen

All of the above are available at your local bookstore,
or may be ordered by contacting Hay House (see next page).

We hope you enjoyed this Hay House Lifestyles book.
If you'd like to receive our online catalog featuring additional information
on Hay House books and products, or if you'd like to find out more
about the Hay Foundation, please contact:

Hay House, Inc., P.O. Box 5100, Carlsbad, CA 92018-5100
(760) 431-7695 or (800) 654-5126
(760) 431-6948 (fax) or (800) 650-5115 (fax)
**www.hayhouse.com®** • **www.hayfoundation.org**

***Published and distributed in Australia by:*** Hay House Australia Pty. Ltd.,
18/36 Ralph St., Alexandria NSW 2015 • *Phone:* 612-9669-4299
*Fax:* 612-9669-4144 • www.hayhouse.com.au

***Published and distributed in the United Kingdom by:*** Hay House UK, Ltd.,
292B Kensal Rd., London W10 5BE • *Phone:* 44-20-8962-1230
*Fax:* 44-20-8962-1239 • www.hayhouse.co.uk

***Published and distributed in the Republic of South Africa by:*** Hay House SA
(Pty), Ltd., P.O. Box 990, Witkoppen 2068 • *Phone/Fax:* 27-11-467-8904
www.hayhouse.co.za

***Published in India by:*** Hay House Publishers India, Muskaan Complex, Plot
No. 3, B-2, Vasant Kunj, New Delhi 110 070 • *Phone:* 91-11-4176-1620
*Fax:* 91-11-4176-1630 • www.hayhouse.co.in

***Distributed in Canada by:*** Raincoast, 9050 Shaughnessy St., Vancouver, B.C.
V6P 6E5 • *Phone:* (604) 323-7100 • *Fax:* (604) 323-2600 • www.raincoast.com

## Take Your Soul on a Vacation

Visit **www.HealYourLife.com®** to regroup, recharge, and reconnect
with your own magnificence. Featuring blogs, mind-body-spirit news,
and life-changing wisdom from Louise Hay and friends.

Visit **www.HealYourLife.com** today!